Public Utility Accounting

Steven M. Bragg

AccountingTools®

ISBN 978-1-64221-143-6

For more information about AccountingTools® products, visit our Web site at www.accountingtools.com.

Table of Contents

About the Author

Steven Bragg, CPA, has been the chief financial officer or controller of four companies, as well as a consulting manager at Ernst & Young. He received a master's degree in finance from Bentley College, an MBA from Babson College, and a Bachelor's degree in Economics from the University of Maine. He has been a two-time president of the Colorado Mountain Club, and is an avid alpine skier, mountain biker, and certified master diver. Mr. Bragg resides in Centennial, Colorado. He has written more than 300 books and courses, including *New Controller Guidebook*, *GAAP Guidebook*, and *Payroll Management*.

Steven maintains the accountingtools.com web site, which contains continuing professional education courses, the Accounting Best Practices podcast, and thousands of articles on accounting subjects.

Buy Additional AccountingTools Courses

AccountingTools offers more than 1,500 hours of CPE courses, with concentrations in accounting, auditing, finance, taxation, and ethics. Related courses that you might like include:

- Activity-Based Costing
- Governmental Accounting

Go to accountingtools.com/cpe to view these additional courses.

AccountingTools®

Public Utility Accounting

Introduction

The proper recordation of accounting information is unusually important in a public utility. This information is needed not just by managers and lenders to make decisions about the business, but also by regulators who are setting the rates it can charge to customers. The latter issue is so critical that a case can be made for the accounting function being one of the most important areas of a public utility.

The accounting for a public utility follows strict guidelines laid down by the Federal Energy Regulatory Commission (FERC), which provides a highly-structured chart of accounts, along with detailed instructions for which transactions are to be recorded within these accounts. By employing such a highly-structured approach to accounting, regulators will know with some confidence that the accounting information from which they are developing rates is reliable.

In this course, we cover the account structure used by a public utility and the accounting for many aspects of capital assets, as well as the accounting for operating expenses, materials and supplies, payroll, bond transactions, and much more.

Overview of Public Utilities

A public utility is a business that furnishes an everyday necessity to the public at large. Public utilities provide electricity, natural gas, telephone service, and other essentials to the public. In this course, we focus on the accounting requirements of an electric utility. There are five main types of electric utilities, which are as follows:

- *Investor-owned utilities*. The largest utilities are usually investor-owned. They are regulated by the state governments, which grant them an exclusive service territory. The applicable government commission authorizes the retail rates that these entities can provide, and also oversee the customer service and equipment maintenance levels of the utilities. These entities primarily provide distribution and transmission services for their customers.

- *Rural electric cooperatives*. These entities provide electricity to rural areas, frequently with very low population densities. Given the financial difficulty of providing service in low-density areas, they do not generate their own power, and are supported by low-cost loans granted by a variety of rural electric programs. They are owned by the incorporated areas within their territories.

- *Municipally-owned utilities*. Municipalities directly own several thousand electric utilities, ranging from quite modest operations to some of the largest utilities in the country. These utilities are usually regulated by the owning municipalities. The smaller municipalities purchase their power from other parties and so are only responsible for distributing it to customers.

- *Independent power producers*. These entities own power production facilities and have a broad array of ownership structures, ranging from private to public ownership. They sell power both to utilities and end users.
- *Power marketers*. These entities operate power generation facilities and transmission lines, and only sell to wholesale distributors, such as rural electric cooperatives and municipally-owned utilities.

Public Utility Accounting Issues

In the following sub-sections, we provide an overview of the general accounting issues faced by a public utility.

Applicable Accounting Standards

An electric utility that is owned by a municipality is part of the local government, and so must generate financial reports in accordance with the accounting framework of the Governmental Accounting Standards Board (GASB). These entities usually conduct their accounting as enterprise funds within the local government entity. An *enterprise fund* is a self-supported government fund that sells goods and services to the public for a fee.

When a utility is privately-owned, it instead generates financial reports in accordance with the Generally Accepted Accounting Principles (GAAP) framework, which is promulgated by the Financial Accounting Standards Board.

Financial Statement Reporting

A utility that operates as an enterprise fund is required to report the following three financial statements:

- *Statement of revenues, expenses and changes in net position*. As the name implies, this report presents all revenues earned and expenses incurred, as well as any capital contributions and transfers made. This format is similar to that of the income statement, which is used by for-profit businesses.
- *Statement of net position*. This report presents the financial position of a government entity. Its format is similar to that of the balance sheet, which is used by for-profit businesses.
- *Statement of cash flows*. This report separately presents four types of cash flows, which are as follows:
  - o *Operating activities*. Several of the cash flows covered are cash receipts from customers, payments to suppliers, payments to employees, and payments for services made to other funds.
  - o *Capital and related financing activities*. Includes the borrowing and repayment of debt related to capital improvements. Since utilities are capital-intensive, this section is heavily used by them.
  - o *Noncapital financing activities*. Includes the borrowing of money for any activity that does not include the acquisition, construction, or

improvement of capital assets, as well as the repayment of these borrowings. A utility will report any payments in lieu of taxes in this section, as well as grants and advances made to other funds.

o *Investing activities*. Includes any expenditures for investment instruments, as well as cash receipts from the sale of these instruments.

This statement of cash flows format is a more complex version of the report used by for-profit businesses (which only presents three types of cash flows).

Expenditure Classifications

One of the essential accounting decisions for an electric utility is deciding whether an expenditure should be classified as a capital expenditure or as an operation and maintenance (O&M) expense. The cost of a capital expenditure is recovered over multiple years through depreciation, while an O&M expense is charged off in the current reporting period.

This decision can have a major impact on the reported results and financial position of a utility. Capitalization of an expenditure results in a reduced impact on profits within the current period, and recovery of the cost through the utility's rate structure over several years. Alternatively, if it is charged to expense in the current period, then the current year's reported income is reduced, but the utility should be able to recover the cost more quickly through its rate structure.

A regulated utility is allowed a certain rate of return on its rate base. This return is designed to give a utility a fixed rate of return on its operating margin (prior to non-operating expenses). The rate base in this calculation is the original cost of a utility's plant, minus its accumulated depreciation. Given the importance of this issue, the accountant needs to be absolutely certain about *which* expenditures are classified as assets, *when* they are classified as such, and the amount of depreciation charged.

Expenditures related to utility operations that are expensed are usually recovered from ratepayers in the current revenue requirement, while expenditures capitalized as assets are instead recovered through its rates as assets are depreciated. To be more specific, a utility's rates are intended to reimburse it for all utility operating expenses incurred. Conversely, a utility's non-operating expenses are not recovered through the rates it charges to customers. Non-operating expenses typically relate to investment income, or gains/losses on the sale of property.

Tip: A utility should clearly define what constitutes an operating activity and a non-operating activity, so that the related expenses can be properly classified as such. This definition may require expansion over time, to incorporate any unusual transactions that could be recorded either way.

Reporting Requirements

The depth of detail that an electric utility needs to compile is generally quite expansive, since it may have to provide a range of reports to multiple regulatory agencies, such as the FERC and the applicable state public service commission. In addition, if a utility has issued debt to the investment community, then it must issue financial reports to the Securities and Exchange Commission, and will have to provide detailed financial information to a credit reporting agency in order to obtain a bond rating.

The Uniform System of Accounts

The Uniform System of Accounts is promulgated by the FERC. Employing a uniform account structure across the industry makes it easier for regulators, governments, lenders, and the investment community to compare the results and financial positions of different utilities. The FERC's official account structure also provides definitions for each account, to reduce any uncertainty about where to record transactions.

Note: The complete text of the Uniform System of Accounts can be found in the Code of Federal Regulations by searching for 7 CFR Subpart B – Uniform System of Accounts. A well-formatted source of this text is located at https://www.law.cornell.edu/cfr/text/18/part-101.

The top-to-bottom structure of the Uniform System of Accounts is as follows:

1. Definitions
2. General Instructions
3. Electric Plant Instructions
4. Operating Expense Instructions
5. Statement of Net Position Chart of Accounts and Descriptions
6. Electric Plant Chart of Accounts and Descriptions
7. Income Chart of Accounts and Descriptions
8. Retained Earnings Chart of Accounts and Descriptions
9. Operating Revenue Chart of Accounts and Descriptions
10. Operation and Maintenance Expense Chart of Accounts and Descriptions

A particular benefit of using the FERC account structure is that it provides guidelines for when an expenditure is to be treated as an expense and when it should be capitalized. This is a major benefit, given the very large capital investments typically made in electricity generation and distribution systems.

The FERC account structure is based on the *activity-based costing* methodology, where costs are linked to specific activities. By using this approach, one can determine the entire cost to conduct each activity, such as electricity generation, meter reading, and customer billings. This information is useful for zeroing in on activities that are incurring excessive costs.

The numbering system used in the FERC chart of accounts employs the same general structure employed by many organizations, with a few adjustments. As usual, the numbering scheme begins with asset and liability accounts, and then proceeds through income and expense accounts. Three-digit account numbering is used in most cases. The general numbering scheme appears in the following exhibit.

FERC Chart of Accounts Numbering Scheme

Account Number Range	Type of Account
100-199	Assets and other debits
200-299	Liabilities and other credits
300-399	Plant accounts
400-432, 434-435	Income accounts
433, 436-439	Retained earnings accounts
440-459	Revenue accounts
500-599	Production, transmission, and distribution expenses
900-949	Customer accounts, customer service and informational, sales, and general and administrative expenses

In the preceding exhibit for the FERC chart of accounts numbering scheme, the 500-series of accounts are considered to be operating costs, and so can be charged through to customers through a utility's rate structure. In the following exhibit, we break down the chart of accounts into greater detail.

Detailed FERC Chart of Accounts

Account Range	Account Type	Account Name
101-120	Balance Sheet | Assets and Other Debits	Utility Plant
121-129	Balance Sheet | Assets and Other Debits	Other Property & Investments
130-174	Balance Sheet | Assets and Other Debits	Current & Accrued Assets
181-190	Balance Sheet | Assets and Other Debits	Deferred Debits
201-216	Balance Sheet | Equities, Liabilities & Other Credits	Proprietary Capital (Equity)
221-226	Balance Sheet | Equities, Liabilities & Other Credits	Long-Term Debt
227-229	Balance Sheet | Equities, Liabilities & Other Credits	Other Concurrent Liabilities
231-243	Balance Sheet | Equities, Liabilities & Other Credits	Current & Accrued Liabilities
251-283	Balance Sheet | Equities, Liabilities & Other Credits	Deferred Credits
301-303	Utility Plant Accounts	Intangible
310-346	Utility Plant Accounts	Production (Electric)
304-347	Utility Plant Accounts	Production (Gas)
350-359	Utility Plant Accounts	Transmission (Electric)
350-364	Utility Plant Accounts	Natural Gas Storage (Gas)
360-373	Utility Plant Accounts	Distribution (Electric)
365-371	Utility Plant Accounts	Transmission (Gas)

Account Range	Account Type	Account Name
374-387	Utility Plant Accounts	Distribution (Gas)
389-399	Utility Plant Accounts	General
400-414	Income Accounts	Utility Operating Income
415-426	Income Accounts	Other Income and Deductions
427-432	Income Accounts	Interest Charges
433	Equity Accounts	Balance Transferred from Income
434-435	Income Accounts	Extraordinary Items
436	Equity Accounts	Appropriations of Retained Earnings
437-438	Equity Accounts	Dividends Declared
439	Equity Accounts	Adjustments to Retained Earnings
440-449	Operating Revenue Accounts	Sales of Electricity
480-485	Operating Revenue Accounts	Sales of Gas
450-456	Operating Revenue Accounts	Other Operating Revenues (Elec.)
487-496	Operating Revenue Accounts	Other Operating Revenues (Gas)
500-557	Operation and Maintenance Expense Accounts	Power Production (Electric)
560-574	Operation and Maintenance Expense Accounts	Transmission (Electric)
580-598	Operation and Maintenance Expense Accounts	Distribution (Electric)
700-813	Operation and Maintenance Expense Accounts	Production (Gas)
814-847	Operation and Maintenance Expense Accounts	Natural Gas Storage (Gas)
850-870	Operation and Maintenance Expense Accounts	Transmission (Gas)
871-895	Operation and Maintenance Expense Accounts	Distribution (Gas)
901-905	Operation and Maintenance Expense Accounts	Customer Accounts
906-910	Operation and Maintenance Expense Accounts	Customer Service and Information
911-917	Operation and Maintenance Expense Accounts	Sales
920-935	Operation and Maintenance Expense Accounts	Administrative and General

Accrual Basis Accounting

A utility should record accounting transactions in accordance with the accrual basis of accounting. Under this approach, revenue is recorded when earned and expenses when incurred. This differs from the cash basis of accounting, where revenue is recorded when cash is received, and expenses when cash is paid out.

An essential element of accrual basis accounting is the matching principle, which states that all expenses related to revenue should be recorded within the same reporting period as the one in which the revenue was recorded. This approach yields a more consistent picture of a utility's profitability, since revenue and expense transactions are paired together. If this were not the case, expenses might be recognized for several months after the associated revenue was recognized, making it exceedingly difficult to determine the true level of profitability of the business. To achieve a proper matching of revenues and expenses, a utility will need to accrue expenses for which a supplier invoice has not yet been received. Similarly, if a utility has prepaid some expenses, it will need to defer their recognition as expenses until the period in which the related revenue is to be recognized.

Note: In the rate making process (as described later in this course), the recognition of costs considered applicable to future rates may be deferred. These deferrals for rate purposes are considered to conform to GAAP.

One of the most common outcomes of the accrual basis of accounting is *depreciation*. This is the ratable reduction of an asset's cost by charging it to expense over the useful life of the asset. This approach is designed to approximately match the expense incurred to the period over which any corresponding revenue will be earned.

A small public power system with rudimentary accounting systems may still use the cash basis of accounting. Doing so will not result in as accurate results as a system using the accrual basis of accounting, but the cash basis is easier to operate, and so may work within the minimal staffing levels typically maintained by these entities.

Asset and Liability Accounts

The Uniform System of Accounts contains a detailed chart of accounts for all components of a utility's statement of net position. A utility's statement of net position reports its financial position as of a specific point in time. The accounts summarized into the statement of net position include all asset, liability, and equity accounts. Asset accounts store monetary information about a company's resources, while liability accounts store all legally binding obligations payable to a third party, and equity accounts are the financial representation of the ownership of a business. Stated differently, equity accounts contain the claims of owners against the net assets of a utility. In cases where a government entity owns a utility, the equity accounts really represent the net asset ownership of the government in the utility. More information about these accounts appears in the following sub-sections. A sample statement of net position for a public utility appears at the end of this section.

Asset Accounts

The four main clusters of assets contained within the Uniform System of Accounts are as follows:

- *Utility plant.* The general types of accounts within the utility plant categorization are electric plant in service, construction work in progress, and the accumulated depreciation and accumulated amortization associated with these accounts. There are other accounts for special circumstances, such as experimental electric plant and electric plant leased to others. There are also several classifications used to record the cost of nuclear fuel in different stages of use. Assets to include in the electric plant accounts include everything used in the generation, transmission, and distribution of electricity, as well as any equipment that supports utility operations.

- *Other property and investments.* The general types of accounts within the other property and investments category are nonutility property, investments in other companies, and several related funds. These accounts are used to record long-term assets that are similar in nature to utility plant. The general orientation of these accounts is toward assets that are held for investment purposes. The fund accounts are used to record cash investments that will be used later, such as for plant replacements.

- *Current and accrued assets.* The general types of accounts within the current and accrued assets category are for assets that will be liquidated in the short term, such as cash, trade receivables, short-term investments, and inventory. Industry-specific accounts found within this classification include fuel stock, nuclear materials held for sale, and accrued utility revenues.

- *Deferred debits.* The general types of accounts within the deferred debits categorization relate to costs that will be dealt with at a later date. For example, a clearing account is used to record a variety of costs, which will be reapportioned and recorded elsewhere at a later date. The operating costs of various types of heavy equipment are initially recorded in a clearing account, after which a portion is charged to expense and the remainder is capitalized into the construction projects on which they are used.

An unusual feature of a utility's statement of net position structure is that it ignores the order of liquidity. The order of liquidity concept states that those elements of the statement that are the most liquid (such as cash) are to be shown first within the assets section, while those liabilities that are to be settled first (such as trade payables) are to be shown first within the liabilities section. However, a utility reports its investment in utility plant first in the assets section, despite it being the least liquid part of its assets. The reason for this alteration in the presentation order is that by far the largest portion of its asset investment is in this area, and so it is presented first.

Liability Accounts

The five main clusters of liabilities contained within the Uniform System of Accounts are as follows:

- *Proprietary capital*. This is the funds and other assets paid in by a utility's shareholders, as well as any undistributed accumulated earnings from its operations. In the case of a publicly-owned utility, there are no funds or assets paid in by shareholders. For a privately-owned utility, this category contains several accounts in which to record shareholder purchases of a firm's common stock and preferred stock. There are also several accounts pertaining to appropriated and unappropriated retained earnings. Appropriated retained earnings have been set aside for specific uses.
- *Long-term debt*. A utility frequently must take on long-term debt in order to pay for long-term assets. Consequently, among the more heavily-used accounts are bonds, unamortized premiums on bonds, and unamortized discounts on bonds.
- *Other noncurrent liabilities*. This category is used to compile a variety of "other" liabilities, such as provisions for injuries, pensions, and asset retirement obligations; essentially any liabilities that are not expected to be paid within the current year.
- *Current and accrued liabilities*. The accounts within this group are expected to be settled within one year. These accounts include trade payables, short-term notes payable, customer deposits, accrued taxes and interest, and declared dividends.
- *Deferred credits*. Deferred credits include those obligations for which a utility is liable, but which are not expected to be paid within the next year. Examples of these accounts are customer advances for construction and accumulated deferred income taxes.

Note: It is quite unlikely that the full range of accounts included in the Uniform System of Accounts will ever be used by a smaller utility. Given their small range of operating and financial activities, these organizations may employ only a small subset of the full range of available accounts.

Sample Statement of Net Position

(Dollars in thousands)	20X1
Assets and Deferred Outflows of Resources	
Non-Current Assets:	
Utility plant	$794,712
Restricted assets	125,372
Other non-current assets	18,425
Total non-current assets	938,509
Current Assets:	
Cash and cash equivalents	324,848
Accounts receivable, less allowance for doubtful accounts	31,222
Accrued interest receivable	1,301
Inventory	1,300
Prepaid expenses	5,839
Public benefit programs	17,280
Total current assets	381,790
Total Assets	1,320,299
Deferred Outflows of Resources:	
Deferred outflows related to pension	22,300
Changes in derivative values	14,740
Loss on refunding	9,623
Total deferred outflow of resources	46,663
Total assets and deferred outflows of resources	1,366,962
Net Position, Liabilities and Deferred Inflows of Resources	
Net investment in capital assets	510,732
Long-term obligations, less current portion	616,130
Other Non-Current Liabilities:	
Net pension liability	85,218
Nuclear decommissioning liability	52,864
Net other post-employment benefits liability	8,572
Derivative instruments	21,941
Total non-current liabilities	168,595
Current Liabilities:	
Accounts payable and other accruals	25,071
Compensated absences	5,206
Customer deposits	7,317
Nuclear decommissioning liability	5,335
Current portion of long-term obligations	12,483

Total current liabilities	55,412
Total liabilities	840,137
Deferred Inflows of Resources:	
Deferred inflows related to pension	16,093
Total Net Position, Liabilities and Deferred Inflows of Resources	$1,366,962

The preceding statement of net position contained several line items pertaining to the deferred inflow and outflow of resources. A *deferred inflow of resources* occurs when there is an acquisition of net assets that applies to a future reporting period. A *deferred outflow of resources* occurs when there is consumption of net assets that applies to a future reporting period. A *resource* is an item that can be drawn down to provide services to citizens. Hedging transactions typically result in deferred inflows or outflows of resources.

EXAMPLE

The Carmel Utility sells some of its property and later leases it back. To properly reflect the full extent of these two transactions, the utility's accounting department reports the $500,000 gain on sale of the property as a deferred inflow of resources, which is amortized over the 20-year life of the lease. This deferred inflow will decline over the life of the lease.

EXAMPLE

The Carmel Utility has a $100,000 gain in the current period that is to be used as an offset to expenses in future periods via an adjustment to its recoverable costs. The utility's accounting department reports this gain as a deferred inflow of resources. This deferred inflow will decline over the recovery period.

Income and Expense Accounts

A utility's statement of revenues, expenses, and changes in net position reports its financial results over a specific date range. The accounts summarized into this statement break down revenues and expenses into finer detail, so that one can discern their specific sources.

At the end of a utility's fiscal year, it transfers the year-to-date net income (or loss) it has generated into the retained earnings account in the statement of net position, thereby clearing out these accounts and preparing them for use again in the following fiscal year.

More information about the income and expense accounts appears in the following sub-sections. A sample statement of revenues, expenses, and changes in net position for a public utility appears at the end of this section.

Utility Operating Income

This cluster of accounts identifies the revenue and expense accounts that are most commonly associated with the basic operations of an electric utility. These accounts are clustered together so that they can be netted, resulting in a net operating income figure for the entity's operations. When a utility is rate regulated, this net operating income figure serves as the dividing line between expenses that regulators will allow to be recovered through its rate structure (operating expenses), and those that are not (non-operating expenses).

The main classification of utility operating income is operating revenues, which is comprised of many sub-accounts. Among the more heavily used sub-accounts are residential sales, commercial and industrial sales, and public street and highway lighting. Lower-volume revenue accounts include rent from electric property, forfeited customer discounts, and revenues from the transmission of electricity.

There are many operating and maintenance expenses in the Uniform System of Accounts. They are broken down into clusters, based on the type of electricity-generating operation. Thus, there is a cluster of operating expense accounts pertaining to steam power generation, another for nuclear power generation, and yet another for hydraulic power generation. A smaller utility might only use the accounts within the other power generation cluster of accounts, which pertain to other sources of power, such as natural-gas power generation. Some of the accounts are unique to a power-generating cluster of expenses, such as nuclear fuel expense for the nuclear power generation cluster. Other accounts are found in all of the clusters, such as operation supervision and engineering, maintenance supervision and engineering, and maintenance of structures. There is also a separate set of accounts relating to customer service and administrative activities. Examples of customer service accounts are meter reading expenses, collection expenses, and advertising expenses. Examples of administrative accounts are administrative and general salaries, property insurance, and regulatory commission expenses.

There are three other clusters of operating expenses that do not relate to power generation – they address transmission expenses, regional market expenses, and distribution expenses. The transmission function covers all plant from the point of generation or receipt of power supply to the entrance to the distribution system. The distribution system includes all other plant required for delivery of power to customers. Examples of transmission and distribution expenses (common to both categories) are load dispatching, overhead line expenses, underground line expenses, and maintenance of structures. Examples of the expense accounts within the regional market expenses cluster are transmission rights market administration, capacity market administration, and market monitoring and compliance.

Other Income and Deductions

This cluster of accounts covers both revenue and expense activities, but not for activities that are part of the normal provision of electric utility service to customers. Examples of these activities are merchandise sales, rental income from property leasing, and the completion of contract services. It also includes financial activities, such as investment income. Examples of these accounts are revenues from merchandising, jobbing, and contract work, interest and dividend income, and donations.

Interest Charges

This cluster of accounts covers the interest costs on short-term and long-term debt that has been issued to finance utility operations. It also covers other expenses associated with debt financing. Examples of these accounts are interest on long-term debt and the amortization of debt discount and expense.

Sample Statement of Revenues, Expenses, and Changes in Net Position

(Dollars in thousands)	
	20X1
Operating Revenues	
Residential sales	$116,303
Commercial sales	69,878
Industrial sales	114,078
Other sales	4,824
Wholesale sales	344
Transmission revenue	35,730
Other operating revenue	13,121
Public benefit programs	9,292
Total operating revenues before uncollectibles	363,570
Estimated uncollectibles, net of bad debt recovery	-911
Total operating revenues, net of uncollectibles	362,659
Operating Expenses	
Production and purchased power	155,264
Transmission	64,443
Distribution	58,729
Public benefit programs	8,933
Depreciation	34,471
Total operating expenses	321,840
Operating Income	40,819
Non-Operating Revenues (Expenses)	
Investment income	13,372
Interest expense and fiscal charges	-25,053
Gain on sale of assets	287
Other	3,989
Total non-operating revenues (expenses)	-7,405
Income before capital contributions and transfers out	33,414

Capital contributions	6,383
Transfers out – contributions to city's general fund	-39,886
Total capital contributions and transfers out	-33,503
Increase in net position	-89
Net Position, Beginning of Year	510,821
Net Position, End of Year	$510,732

Capital Asset Accounting

One of the most important aspects of public utility accounting relates to capital assets. The accounting for them must address which costs to include in constructed assets, how to deal with contributed assets, the capitalization of interest, the use of retirement units, how to calculate depreciation, and whether asset impairment exists. These topics and more are covered in the following sub-sections.

Capital Assets

A capital asset is property that is expected to generate value over a long period of time. Capital assets form the productive base of a utility. Examples of capital assets are generators, transformers, trucks, and computer equipment. Utilities are highly asset-intensive, so they invest a large part of their funds in capital assets. A capital asset has the following characteristics:

- It has an expected useful life of more than one year.
- Its acquisition cost exceeds a company-designated minimum amount, known as the capitalization limit.
- It is not expected to be sold as a normal part of business operations.
- It tends not to be easily convertible into cash.

Note: A special characteristic of nuclear power plant operation is that nuclear fuel is accounted for as a fixed asset, because of its long useful life. This means that the cost of the fuel should be depreciated over its estimated useful life. The depreciation rate is calculated based on the total cost of the fuel in a reactor, and the estimated energy to be generated by that fuel.

Once nuclear fuel has been depleted, it may (among other options) be stored using dry-cask storage. These storage costs should be accrued as the fuel is used, so that the full cost of using the fuel is recognized during the periods when it is generating energy.

Contributed Assets

A public utility may receive contributed assets, which are goods and services received with no payment made in exchange. These transfers are usually made by the owning municipality, and take the form of land, buildings, equipment, and materials. These assets should be shown by the utility as capital contributions in its stand-alone financial statements. The assets are instead reported as transfers in the governing entity's government-wide financial statements.

Accounting for Electric Plant Costs

The instructions for the Uniform System of Accounts are quite specific about how to account for the costs of an electric plant. The more important accounting issues are as follows:

- *Cost of plant.* The cost of an electric plant must be recorded at the cost at which it was originally placed in service. Thus, a facility acquired from another utility must be recorded at the cost to the originating utility. Also, any contributions received toward the cost of the facility must be charged against (reducing) its costs.
- *Costs to include.* The costs to assign to an asset include all costs associated with its construction or purchase, as well as the costs incurred to prepare it for use. The costs most likely to be included are materials and supplies, labor, and transportation costs. These costs may come from materials issuances from inventory, employee compensation, and the use of company equipment and vehicles. Other ancillary costs to include are the costs of studies, permits, site security, training costs, and insurance.
- *Engineering and supervision.* The costs of engineering and supervision that relate to construction projects are to be capitalized into those projects. Where it is difficult to do so on a recurring basis, a periodic study could be used instead to develop an apportionment percentage.
- *General and administration.* That portion of the compensation and other expenses of a utility's officers and administrative staff relating to construction projects should be capitalized into those projects. Where it is difficult to do so on a recurring basis, a periodic study could be used instead to develop an apportionment percentage.

EXAMPLE

A utility incurs $500,000 of compensation and expenses for its engineering and administrative staff. Based on a time study that is conducted annually, 40% of the labor of these people is attributable to capital construction projects. Consequently, $200,000 of this overhead cost (calculated as $500,000 × 40%) should be assigned to capital projects. In the current year, $6,000,000 is spent on capital projects. Therefore, an overhead charge rate of 3.33% (calculated as $200,000 ÷ $6,000,000) should be charged for each dollar of costs assigned to a capital project in the current year.

Note: When capital projects span multiple accounting periods (a common occurrence), a new overhead rate will be applied to the cost incurred in each period, based on the latest compilation of the overhead charge rate.

- *Interest cost*. The cost of borrowed funds during the construction period should be capitalized into the cost of electric plant. This also includes a reasonable rate on other funds that are used to construct the facility. This issue is addressed further in a later sub-section.
- *Overhead allocation*. All overhead costs associated with electric plant construction must be charged to individual plant jobs or units, which requires the use of a consistently-applied allocation methodology. This can be achieved with an occasional allocation analysis that is then used for subsequent overhead allocations.

Work Orders

Unique work orders must be established for all construction and asset retirement projects, so that costs can be properly collected for each one. Job orders may be used instead to track the costs associated with smaller recurring capital projects.

Work orders are an essential source document, since they show the detail for how costs were accumulated for the project with which they are paired. This information is used by regulators to develop equitable utility rates.

When a work order is associated with a project that is expected to benefit more than one period or increase the useful life of an asset, then the accumulated costs are recorded in the relevant asset account. If a work order is instead associated with maintenance activities, then the accumulated costs are charged to expense in the period to which the costs relate.

There should also be an underlying accounting system that accumulates the costs associated with each work order, the origins of those costs, and the accounts to which these amounts have been charged. For example, employees include the appropriate work order number on their time sheets when charging their time to a capital project. Any purchases made from outside parties would be charged to the work order number through the accounts payable system.

Tip: Do not take the time to charge immaterial amounts to capital projects, such as the time of payables clerks in regard to project-specific supplier invoices. The effort to do so is too great in relation to the increased level of accuracy obtained.

During a construction project that is to be capitalized, costs are accumulated to a work order and then closed to the construction work on progress (CWIP) account at the end of each fiscal year. The CWIP account is a temporary holding location for accumulated costs. The work order will remain open and will continue to accumulate costs until all costs related to the project have been incurred and the resulting assets are placed into service. At that time, all costs are shifted from the CWIP account to the most applicable plant asset account.

The costs incurred to retire an asset from use must be tracked separately from the cost to construct it. This calls for the use of a separate work order for asset construction and a separate work order for asset retirement. Thus, when an asset is being replaced, a retirement work order should be issued for the work required to take out the old asset, while another work order is issued to accumulate the costs of the new asset. Retirement costs include expenditures to demolish or dismantle facilities, including all associated transport costs. Given the types of activities involved, the costs charged to retirement work orders typically involve large amounts of labor, as well as transport and equipment costs.

EXAMPLE

The Eldora Electric Power Company issues retirement work order number 5296 to remove certain overhead distribution facilities, and construction work order number 3178 to install replacement equipment. The following table itemizes the costs associated with each of these work orders.

Work Order #	Description	Units	Price per Unit	Material Cost	Labor per Unit	Labor Cost
3178	Pole	4	$250.00	$1,000.00	$125.00	$500.00
3178	Conductor	500	0.75	375.00	1.00	500.00
3178	Anchor	1	24.00	24.00	75.00	75.00
3178	Transformer	1	3,600.00	3,600.00	225.00	225.00
	Totals			**$4,999.00**		**$1,300.00**
5296	Transformer	1	--	--	--	$60.00
5296	Cutout	1	--	--	--	25.00
5296	Arrestor	1	--	--	--	30.00
	Totals					**$115.00**

The total expenditure across both work orders is $6,414. The company has an overhead charge rate of 5%. When applied to the $6,414 of direct costs incurred, this adds $321 to their cost, resulting in a total burdened cost of $6,735.

There may be cases in which people working on an asset retirement find that they can salvage materials or equipment that can be re-used by the utility or perhaps even sold off to others. When these items are retained for in-house use, they are first returned to the warehouse. When these items are sold off, the amount recognized from their sale is the amount paid to the utility, minus any expenses associated with the sale.

Allowance for Funds Used

Another cost of a capital project is the allowance for funds used during construction. This allowance determines the amount of funding costs that can be capitalized into the cost of a project. This is an imputed cost, since it is assumed that a utility is providing the funding for its capital projects from its general store of funds, and not from a specific financing instrument. The maximum amount of interest that can be capitalized is set by a complex FERC formula that is contained within electric plant instruction number 3.17 of the Uniform System of Accounts. This formula takes into account all of a utility's cost of financing, including the costs of its long-term debt, short-term debt, and common equity.

> **Note:** Because some financing costs are being capitalized into the cost of capital projects, this effectively increases the profits reported by a utility in the current period. The capitalized financing costs will be recognized in later periods, when they are charged to expense through depreciation.

There are a few standard rules that utilities follow when capitalizing financing costs. They are as follows:

- There is no financing capitalization unless a project is expected to have a duration of more than 30 days, thereby eliminating any financing capitalizations for minor projects.
- There is no financing capitalization when assets are purchased – only when they are constructed.
- Only half of the regular capitalization rate is applied to current month expenditures, on the grounds that these expenditures were only outstanding for part of the month.
- There is no financing capitalization during periods when construction has stopped for an extended period of time.

Recordation of Asset Costs

When a power-generating facility is being constructed, its cost is assigned to the *Construction Work in Progress* account. Once the facility is placed in service and is providing power to customers, the balance in the account is shifted over to the *Electric Plant in Service* account. Only the balances in the *Electrical Plant in Service* account are depreciated; CWIP is not depreciated. The same approach applies to other types of capital assets.

The exact type of asset tracking used depends on the type of asset. Within a utility, it is not practical to individually track specific assets, such as poles and conductors. These assets are homogenous and interchangeable. Accordingly, these *mass assets* are tracked as groups of assets. Another group of assets is *non-mass assets*, which are specifically identifiable, and so can be tracked separately; examples are substations and generating facilities. Finally, *special units* are assets that require special accounting treatment, because of regulatory requirements or industry practice; for example, meters and transformers are capitalized before they are placed into service.

> **Note:** There is no general FERC recommendation for the capitalization threshold, above which an expenditure should be capitalized. Instead, the FERC regulations are very specific about which expenditures are to be capitalized, no matter what they cost.

When assets are retired, their costs and associated amounts of accumulated depreciation are removed from the accounting records, along with any gain or loss on the retirement.

Retirement Units

When work orders are completed and costs are assigned to specific capital assets, the costs collected under these work orders are assigned to specific assets, which are known as retirement units. A *retirement unit* is an asset whose book cost will be deducted from a utility's accounts when it is retired. When more than one retirement unit is being constructed under a work order, costs are assigned to each unit on some logical basis, such as direct charges to each unit or as allocations of total project costs.

EXAMPLE

Following the completion of work order 3178 as described in the preceding example, each pole is defined as a retirement unit, as is the 500 feet of conductor. To arrive at the full cost of these units, the $375 cost of each individual pole (the sum of their material and labor cost) is multiplied by the 5% overhead charge rate to arrive at a cost of $393.75.

To arrive at the full cost of the conductor retirement unit, we multiply its $875 direct cost (derived in the same manner) by the same overhead charge rate to arrive at a cost of $918.75.

The maintenance of retirement unit records calls for a recordkeeping system that tracks the cost of each retirement unit, as well as the addition and retirement of each individual retirement unit. The system needs to maintain the information required for any major fixed asset, including its description, location, in-service date, and cost. See the following discussion of continuing property records.

It is also possible to record retirement units as groups when they are of relatively low cost and it is not cost-effective to track them on an individual basis (i.e., mass units). When this is done, the assets are described in the accounting records by quantity brought into service each year, as well as the average cost per unit.

Continuing Property Records

Continuing property records (CPRs) are a perpetual record of a plant in service. A utility's CPRs should generally contain the following information:

- Description and identifying number
- FERC account to which a unit is assigned
- The number of units
- The average cost of units added for each year (vintage)
- The number of surviving units
- The location

CPRs provide a complete set of supporting information by plant account of the quantities and types of property included in each account. This information is also used to calculate depreciation expense by account, as well as to determine when assets need to be replaced.

Intangible Assets

An intangible asset lacks physical substance, is a nonfinancial asset, and has a useful life extending over more than one reporting period. An example of an intangible asset is commercially available computer software that has been purchased or licensed by a utility. Another intangible asset type commonly found in utilities is the rights of way for transmission lines. Intangible assets are treated like other capital assets, except that the related depreciation is renamed amortization. The following additional points regarding intangible assets may apply:

- *Recognition in the financial statements.* Recognize the asset in the statement of net position only if it is identifiable. This is the case when the asset can be separated from the utility and sold or transferred, or the asset arises from legal rights, even if those rights are not separable from the utility or transferable.
- *Recognition of internally developed assets.* When an intangible asset has been internally generated, outlays related to the development of that asset can only be capitalized when all of the following apply:
  o An objective has been stated for the project, as well as the nature of the service capacity expected when the project has been completed;
  o The feasibility of the project has been demonstrated; and
  o The utility can demonstrate that it has the intention, ability, and presence of effort to complete the project.

EXAMPLE

A utility wants to allocate funds toward the development of a patent that can spot fires caused by sparks from transmission lines, using drones equipped with highly sensitive thermal emission scanners. The preceding sentence is a clearly-stated objective for the project.

To continue with the example, the nature of the service capacity is to improve the allocation of firefighting teams to areas where a forest fire is most likely to be triggered by transmission lines.

The utility has made a budgetary commitment to fund the project and entered into contracts with several producers of thermal imaging devices to construct a demonstration unit. The utility has also assigned a manager and support team to the project, and contacted its legal department in regard to securing patent protection for the scanning system.

- *Recognition of new computer software.* When a utility internally develops computer software or uses a third-party contractor to do so, it can capitalize the costs of the software based on the following stages of project completion:

- o *Preliminary project stage.* This stage includes conducting a user needs analysis, determining system requirements, evaluating alternatives and the existence of required technologies, supplier selection, and consultant selection. Outlays for this stage should be charged to expense as incurred.
- o *Application development stage.* This stage includes software coding, installation and testing. Outlays for this stage should be capitalized. The training of employees involved with developing internally generated software is not considered part of the application development stage.
- o *Post-implementation/operation stage.* This stage includes application training and software maintenance. Data conversion is part of this stage, but can be classified as part of the application development stage if doing so is necessary for making the software operational. Outlays for this stage should be charged to expense as incurred.
- o *Recognition of software updates.* Outlays for the modification of computer software that is already operating can be capitalized if the result is an increase in software functionality, an increase in software efficiency, or an extension of the useful life of the software. If none of these improvements occur, the outlays are instead charged to expense.

Note: A utility's website is considered computer software, and so can be capitalized as an intangible asset.

- *Useful life.* The useful life of an intangible asset should not exceed any legal or contractual limitations. The renewal period of an intangible asset should be considered when determining its useful life, since the useful life can encompass several renewal periods. An intangible asset can have an indefinite useful life when there are no legal, regulatory, technological, or other factors that might otherwise limit its useful life. An example of an asset having an indefinite life is a permanent right-of-way easement. When an intangible asset is deemed to have an indefinite life, it is not amortized. If an asset with an indefinite life is later reclassified as having a definite lifespan, it should be amortized from the reclassification date.

Note: Interest can be capitalized on the development of internally generated intangible assets by enterprise funds.

- *Business process reengineering.* A common occurrence is for business process reengineering to occur as part of a software development project, since processes can be altered to fit changes in the new software. Even though these activities may be closely intertwined, the accounting for reengineering work is to charge these costs to expense as incurred. The reason for the differing treatment is that process reengineering involves the redeployment of existing resources, rather than the creation of a new resource.

- *Interface costs*. A utility may incur costs to modify existing software so that it can interface with a new computer system. If this outlay increases the functionality or efficiency of the existing software or extends its estimated useful life, then this cost can be capitalized. If not, the costs are assumed to have been incurred for standard maintenance activities, and are charged to expense as incurred.
- *Legal defense outlays*. A utility may need to expend funds for assistance to defend its legal rights pertaining to an intangible asset. A legal defense of rights does not extend the useful life of the asset, nor does it add any capacity. Therefore, this cost is charged to expense as incurred. However, a different type of legal cost *can* be capitalized – when outlays are incurred to initially register an intangible asset, as would be the case with a patent filing.
- *Maintenance contract*. Utilities routinely enter into annual software maintenance agreements with suppliers, where they pay a fee in exchange for maintenance services and upgrades. Theoretically, the portion of these agreements associated with software upgrades that increase the functionality or efficiency of the software can be capitalized. However, it is generally easier to establish a policy under which maintenance fees are charged to expense as incurred.

Depreciation

Capitalizing costs into assets means that the recognition of these costs has been deferred to a later period. This recognition is then accomplished through the process of depreciation, where costs are written off in a systematic manner over the expected useful life of an asset. Doing so is presumed to match depreciation expenses with the revenues generated by these assets.

Depreciation is calculated by subtracting the estimated salvage value of an asset from its carrying amount on the books of the utility and then spreading the residual cost over the useful life of the asset. Utilities normally use the straight-line depreciation method, where the same amount of depreciation is charged in each year of an asset's useful life.

The problem with this calculation is that the eventual salvage value is a guess, especially for assets that will not be retired for many years. Accordingly, it may be necessary to revisit the salvage value repeatedly over the life of an asset and adjust it as better information becomes available. This may mean that the periodic depreciation rate charged will vary over time.

In cases where there is a significant expected cost associated with removing an asset when it is retired, this expected removal cost can be included in the cost of an asset that is being depreciated. As was the case with salvage value, it may be necessary to periodically adjust the expected removal cost estimate, which in turn will alter the amount of depreciation charged in each period. Since the removal cost will only be incurred after the useful life of an asset has been reached, this means that the asset will have a negative *book value* (which is the original asset cost minus accumulated depreciation). The amount by which the accumulated depreciation exceeds the original asset cost will be the estimated removal cost that was built into the depreciation calculation. When the removal cost is actually incurred, it is charged to the accumulated depreciation account.

EXAMPLE

A utility originally acquired a diesel generator for $650,000. At the time it was originally recorded by the utility's accounting department, it was assumed to have a useful life of 40 years, and to have a salvage value of $30,000 at the end of that time. In addition, the eventual removal of the generator was expected to cost $60,000. Based on this information, the annual depreciation rate for the generator was calculated as follows:

($650,000 purchase cost + $60,000 removal cost - $30,000 salvage value) ÷ 40-year life

= $17,000/year

After 25 years, the utility's managers conclude that this generator must be replaced with one that has greater generating capacity, given the expansion of the local population. The utility is able to sell the old generator to a nearby municipality for $180,000, and pays the expected $60,000 removal cost.

After 25 years, the accumulated depreciation that had built up on the generator was $425,000, against which was charged the $60,000 removal cost. When the accounting department reverses the original $650,000 generator cost and the net accumulated depreciation of $365,000 to clear these items from the books of the utility, the difference is a loss of $285,000, which is then offset against the actual $180,000 salvage value to arrive at a loss of $105,000.

Asset Impairment

Utility assets may be classified as impaired, in which case some or all of their carrying amounts must be written off. Capital assets should be evaluated for impairment when there are events or changes in circumstances indicating that the service utility of an asset may have significantly and unexpectedly declined. These events or changes were not expected to occur when the asset was initially acquired. The *service utility* of an asset is the usable capacity that it was expected to provide when it was acquired. The current usable capacity of an asset may be less than its original usable capacity due to a variety of impairment events, which include physical damage or obsolescence, as well as the enactment of laws that limit its use. The process for determining whether a capital asset is impaired follows these steps:

1. *Identify potential impairments.* A potential impairment should be conspicuous or known to the utility, so there is no need to perform additional steps to identify additional potential impairment events. When an impairment is considered to be temporary, the asset should not be written down. Some of the more common indicators of impairment are:

- o Physical damage to the asset
- o Enactment of laws that impact asset usage
- o Evidence of obsolescence
- o A change in the manner of use of an asset
- o Construction stoppage

EXAMPLE

Due to a funding shortfall, the Halifax Utility has stopped using a warehouse, which is a change in the manner of use of the asset. This can be considered impairment of the asset. Halifax has also stopped the development of software for resource management, which can be considered a construction stoppage, and is therefore also an asset impairment. Further, a new law mandates upgrades to its pollution control equipment, for which it has no available funding. This last item can be considered asset impairment due to the enactment of a law.

EXAMPLE

A coastal utility runs a data processing center that is currently operating near its maximum capacity. A staff person is about to conclude a special project for offshore wind modeling that will cut the usage rate of the data processing center in half. This decline in demand should not be considered evidence of asset obsolescence, since the user was involved in a one-time project.

---

2. *Test for impairment.* If the first step indicates that there are one or more potential impairment conditions present, the accountant should proceed with a test for impairment, where both of the following factors must be present:

- o There is a significant decline in service utility, where expenses are now too high in relation to the benefit obtained from the asset.
- o The decline in service utility was unexpected, where the circumstances of the impairment are not part of the normal life cycle of the asset.

When there is no expectation that an impaired asset will continue to be used, it should be reported at the lower of its carrying value or fair value. When an asset is impaired because construction on it has stopped, the asset should also be reported at the lower of its carrying value or fair value.

Note: When an impairment test indicates that asset impairment has not occurred, the accountant should still reevaluate the remaining estimated useful life and salvage value of the asset, which may result in a change in the remaining periodic depreciation charges against the asset.

For illustrative purposes, the preceding discussion is summarized in the following flowchart.

Decision Process for an Asset Impairment Situation

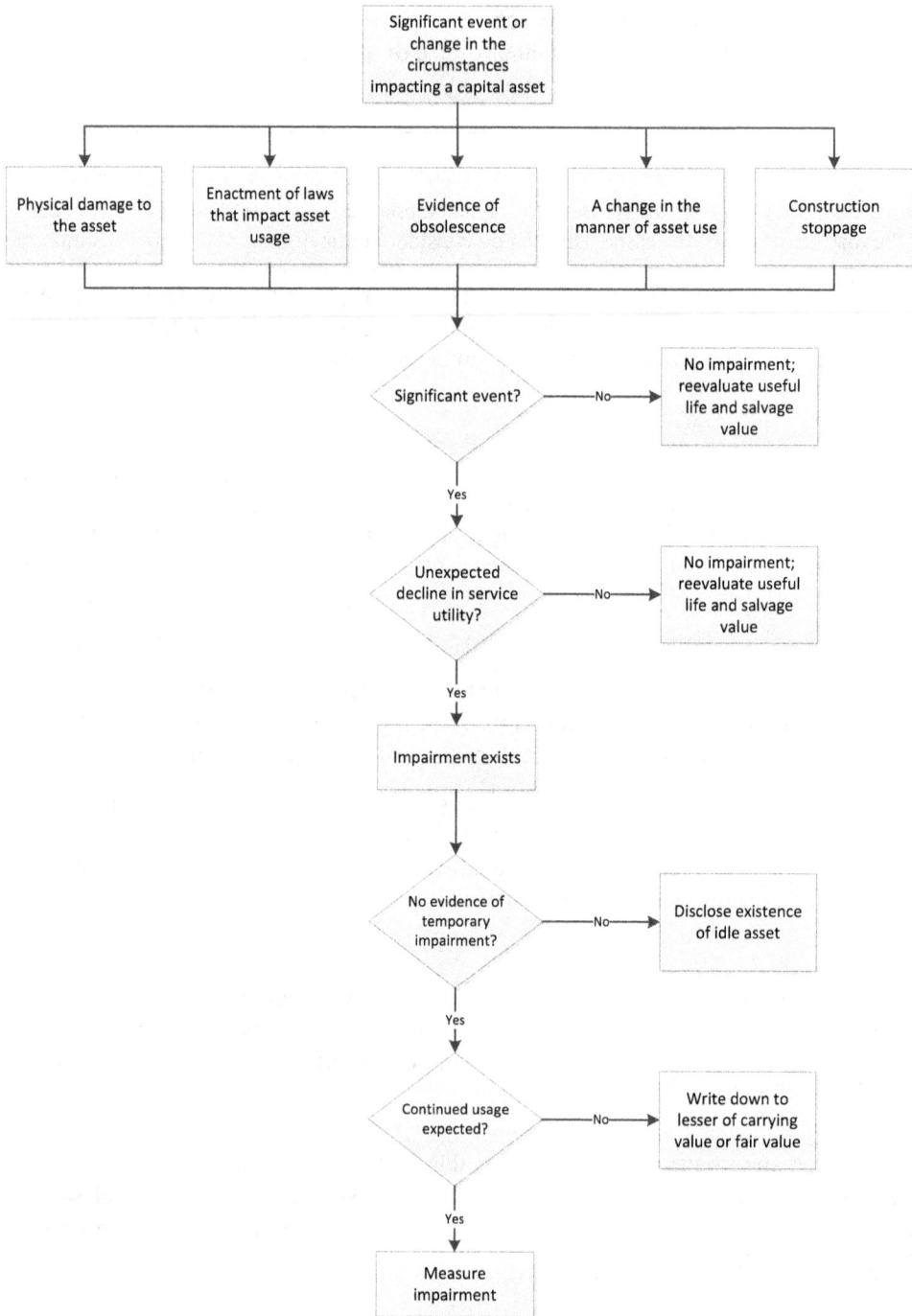

```
┌─────────────────────┐
│ Significant event or │
│     change in the    │
│    circumstances     │
│ impacting a capital  │
│        asset         │
└─────────────────────┘
```

| Physical damage to the asset | Enactment of laws that impact asset usage | Evidence of obsolescence | A change in the manner of asset use | Construction stoppage |

Significant event? —No→ No impairment; reevaluate useful life and salvage value

Yes

Unexpected decline in service utility? —No→ No impairment; reevaluate useful life and salvage value

Yes

Impairment exists

No evidence of temporary impairment? —No→ Disclose existence of idle asset

Yes

Continued usage expected? —No→ Write down to lesser of carrying value or fair value

Yes

Measure impairment

If it is decided that impairment is present, the next issue is determining how much of the asset's historical cost should be written off. The following three methods are available for doing so, where the method chosen should best reflect the decline in service utility of the asset:

- *Restoration cost approach.* This is the cost that would be incurred to restore the utility of the asset. Impairments resulting from physical damage should use this approach.
- *Service units approach.* This is the cost associated with the decline in utility of the asset, which is derived by evaluating the change in maximum estimated service units for the asset, both before and after the impairment event. Impairments resulting from changes in laws, environmental factors, or obsolescence should use this approach.
- *Deflated depreciated replacement cost approach.* This is a derivation of the cost of an asset needed to replace the current level of service, which is then depreciated to reflect its presumed usage and then deflated to convert the asset to its historical cost. Impairments resulting from a change in the manner or duration of use should use this approach.

EXAMPLE

Okie City Utility's spare parts warehouse has been heavily damaged by a tornado. The building was constructed 10 years ago for $3 million, including $200,000 to purchase the underlying land. The warehouse has an expected useful life of 50 years. Fixing the tornado damage will cost $800,000. The capitalization policy of the utility states that 25% of the rebuilding cost is allocated to demolition and scrap removal and 75% to rebuilding the structure. The estimated replacement cost of the facility is $4.5 million.

The calculation of the impairment loss, using the **restoration cost approach**, is:

	Historical Cost	Estimated Useful Life	Accumulated Depreciation	Current Carrying Amount
Land	$200,000			
Building construction	2,800,000	50 years	$560,000	$2,240,000
Total reconstruction cost	800,000			
Percentage rebuilding cost	× 75%			
Restoration cost (current $)	600,000			
Replacement cost (current $)	4,500,000			
Restoration cost ratio	× 13.333%			
Current carrying amount	2,240,000			
Impairment loss	$298,666			

EXAMPLE

A utility built a small coal-fired power plant five years ago, spending $14 million on it. The power plant was originally expected to have a useful life of 50 years. A new federal regulation mandates that the power plant be replaced with an alternative form of power generation that emits less carbon dioxide. The new regulation goes into effect in five years. The existing power plant is impaired due to the adoption of a new regulation, which has altered the service potential of the asset from 50 years to 10 years.

The calculation of the impairment loss, employing the **service units approach**, is:

Historical cost	$14,000,000
Total service units in years	50
Cost per service unit	$280,000
Number of service units made unusable by regulation	× 40
Impairment loss	$11,200,000

EXAMPLE

The Minnow City Utility built offices for its administrative staff five years ago, at a cost of $4 million. Since then, the utility has suffered a catastrophic and permanent decline in revenues, resulting in 80% of its staff being laid off. The decline was due to the closure of several area mines, which had been the primary users of the electricity that the utility generated.

As a result, the offices have been converted into a storage facility for the utility. The offices were originally planned to have a life of 40 years. The current replacement cost for a warehouse of the same dimensions is $1.2 million. A commercial construction index was at 100 when the offices were constructed, and is now at 112.

The calculation of the impairment loss, using the **deflated depreciated replacement cost approach**, is:

Historical cost	$4,000,000
Accumulated depreciation (5 ÷ 40 years)	-500,000
Carrying amount	$3,500,000
Replacement cost of warehouse	$1,200,000
Accumulated depreciation (5 ÷ 40 years)	-150,000
Depreciated replacement cost	$1,050,000
Original commercial construction index	100
Current period commercial construction index	112
Deflation factor	0.89286
Deflated depreciated replacement cost	$937,503
Impairment loss	$2,562,497

There are two possible ways to include the effects of an asset impairment in a capital asset account. These approaches are:

- Increase the accumulated depreciation account by the amount of the loss. This approach treats the impairment as though additional years of useful life have been used up.
- Proportionally reduce the capital asset account and the accumulated depreciation account so that the net decrease in the two accounts equals the impairment loss. This approach treats the impairment as though a portion of the asset has been disposed of.

Once an asset impairment has been recognized, it should not be reversed at a later date, even if the circumstances have changed and there is no ongoing evidence of asset impairment.

Asset Retirement Obligations

Many utilities must incur a significant expenditure to retire some of their assets due to existing laws, statutes, ordinances, contracts, and so forth. This is a particular concern for those owning nuclear reactors, where the retirement costs can run into the hundreds of millions of dollars. The cost of this retirement liability is known as an *asset retirement obligation*. A utility must record a liability in the amount of the present value of this retirement obligation in the period in which the obligation is incurred.

This cost is depreciated over the useful life of the related asset that gives rise to the obligation. Thus, if the ARO is for a nuclear facility that has a useful life of 30 years, then the ARO should be depreciated for 30 years.

The present value of an ARO is based on the best estimate of the current value of the outlays required to remediate the targeted property. This best estimate is based on a probability weighting of all possible outcomes. In the absence of sufficient information, a most likely obligation amount should be used. Further, the amount of the ARO must be reconsidered at least annually, which may result in a series of ongoing adjustments that are treated as separate liability layers.

The amount of this ARO liability is charged to expense over the useful life of the underlying asset through accretion expense. *Accretion expense* is the ongoing, scheduled recognition of an expense related to a long-term liability. The amount charged to expense represents the change in the remaining discounted cash flows of the liability.

EXAMPLE

Glow Atomic is compiling the cost of a decontamination ARO several years in the future for its nuclear facility. It is uncertain of the cost, since supplier fees fluctuate considerably. It arrives at an expected weighted average cash flow based on the following probability analysis:

Cash Flow Estimates	Probability Assessment	Expected Cash Flows
$12,500,000	10%	$1,250,000
15,000,000	15%	2,250,000
16,000,000	50%	8,000,000
22,500,000	25%	5,625,000
	Weighted average cash flows	$17,125,000

The $17.125 million amount is recorded as a liability in account 230, Asset Retirement Obligations.

EXAMPLE

Glow Atomic has been operating an atomic power plant for several years. In the fifth year, Glow detects groundwater contamination, and recognizes an additional layer of ARO liability for $20 million to deal with it. In the seventh year, a leak in the sodium cooling lines causes overheating and a significant release of radioactive steam that impacts 50 square miles of land downwind from the facility. Glow recognizes an additional layer of ARO liability of $150 million to address this issue.

In order to have sufficient cash on hand to pay for an ARO, a utility's oversight board should increase its rates by the amount of the annual ARO amortization. The cash flow generated by this increase is then stored in a reserve account, for use when the obligation must be settled.

The actual amount required to settle the obligation following the end of the useful life of the underlying asset is likely to be somewhat different from the amount accrued for it through ARO accounting. Any difference between the two figures should be accounted for as either a gain (when the actual expenditure is less than the ARO) or a loss (when the actual expenditure is more than the ARO).

Materials and Supplies Inventory

When materials and supplies are initially ordered from suppliers, the eventual disposition of these items may not be known, so it is not possible to charge them to a capital asset or expense account. Instead, the initial purchase transaction is recorded in account 154, *Plant Materials and Operating Supplies*. Depending on the inventory tracking and costing system in use, a utility will track each item on hand and record its cost using the average cost method, first-in first-out method, or whatever other cost tracking system is acceptable under generally accepted accounting principles. Several other costing issues are addressed in the following sub-sections.

Costing of Materials and Supplies

The most common cost tracking method used by utilities is the average costing method. Under this approach, the total cost of all units on hand for a specific item is divided by the total number of units on hand to arrive at the average cost per unit. Then, when one of these items is issued from stock, the inventory value on hand is reduced by this average cost per unit issued. The average cost of the issued item is then shifted to the operating or capital account relating to how the item was used.

EXAMPLE

A rural electric utility has 200 wood poles in stock, for which it paid $50,000. The average cost of these poles is therefore $250. It then purchases an additional 40 poles for $10,400, or $260 each. The average cost of the 240 poles is now $251.67 (calculated as $60,400 ÷ 240 poles). The utility then issues 72 poles from stock. The cost of the issued poles is $18,120 (calculated as $251.67 × 72 poles), leaving a total on-hand cost for the remaining 168 poles of $42,280 (calculated as $251.67 × 168 poles).

The accountant charges the $18,120 cost of the issued poles to account 593, *Maintenance of Overhead Lines*.

Materials Loadings

Materials costs may be loaded with related costs that cannot be easily charged directly to certain types of activities. These loadings are usually associated with low-cost inventory items. The typical inventory of a utility contains thousands of low-cost items. Given their low cost, the warehouse staff may not track them on an individual basis, preferring to instead record their cost in aggregate in account 154, *Plant Materials and Operating Supplies*. The costs in this account are then allocated to the same accounts to which materials issuances are charged.

Materials costs can also be loaded with a utility's stores expense, which is comprised of all costs associated with owning and managing inventory. These costs include the labor for receiving, putaways, and inventory issuances, as well as warehouse operating costs and materials procurement costs. Stores costs are recorded in account 163, *Stores Expense Undistributed*.

The materials loading calculation is based on the proportion of the total costs in accounts 154 and 163 to the total cost of the materials issued during a prior date range (such as the last quarter). These proportions are then multiplied by the cost of issued materials in the current period to arrive at the amount of the loadings.

EXAMPLE

A utility applies the costs of low-cost inventory and stores expense to its maintenance accounts based on the actual proportions of these costs in the preceding year, when they were 4% and 13% of maintenance costs, respectively. The materials loading for four of the maintenance accounts appears in the following table.

Account	Description	Amount	Low-Cost Inventory Items Load (4%)	Stores Expense (13%)	Loaded Amount
591	Maintenance of structures	$18,200	$728	$2,366	$21,294
592	Maintenance of station equipment	4,700	188	611	5,499
593	Maintenance of overhead lines	6,300	252	819	7,371
594	Maintenance of underground lines	10,800	432	1,404	12,636
	Totals	$40,000	$1,600	$5,200	$46,800

Transportation and Equipment Usage

A utility employs a large amount of transportation and other powered equipment, such as cars, trucks, backhoes, and cranes. The ongoing costs of this equipment include batteries, depreciation, engine overhauls, gas, insurance, licensing, repairs, oil, scheduled maintenance, taxes, and tires.

The structure of and usage descriptions for the FERC chart of accounts mandate that the cost of this equipment be allocated to the activities in which the assets are employed. This is usually done by initially storing the costs in a clearing account, which is account 184, *Clearing Accounts*. A utility then periodically allocates these costs out to various activities based on a logical method of allocation. The basis of allocation is usually some measure of equipment usage, such as the number of miles that a truck has been driven during the cost accumulation period. Another option is tracking the number of hours that equipment has been used. In either case, a usage log will need to be maintained in order to develop the basis of allocation.

EXAMPLE

A heavy truck is used for a variety of activities within the maintenance department of a utility. Based on the truck's usage log for the past quarter, it was used for 114 hours on maintenance supervision, 212 hours on maintenance of structures, and 174 hours on maintenance of station equipment. During that time, its associated costs were $1,420. Based on the usage log, the proportion of the $1,420 to be assigned to the maintenance and supervision account is 23%, while the proportion for the maintenance of structures is 42%, with the remaining 35% going to the maintenance of station equipment. This results in the following journal entry:

Account	Account Description	Debit	Credit
590	Maintenance supervision and engineering	327	
591	Maintenance of structures	596	
592	Maintenance of station equipment	497	
184	Clearing accounts		1,420

A potential problem with using the allocation method described in the preceding example is that equipment costs tend to be lumpy, with major expenditures (such as repairs) only occurring at infrequent and unpredictable intervals. This can result in disproportionate cost allocations in periods when these large expenditures occur. To minimize the issue, consider only conducting allocations from the clearing account at longer intervals, such as once a quarter or half-year.

Tip: To further segregate costs, it can make sense to set up sub-accounts within account 184 for different types of transportation and other powered equipment. For example, there might be separate accounts for cars, light trucks, heavy trucks, and backhoes. Each equipment type is more likely to be used for specific activities, so this approach represents a better allocation of costs to activities.

Payroll Accounting

If a utility is using the FERC chart of accounts, it should have a time tracking system in place for compiling the payroll costs associated with the actual hours worked on specific activities – because that is how the chart of accounts is set up. This is especially important in a utility, since the hours worked by employees may end up being charged to an operating or non-operating expense account, or a capital account – each of which has a different impact on the rates charged by the utility. This is of particular importance, because the typical utility incurs a substantial labor cost.

Tip: It can be excessively time-consuming to track hours worked by activity. If so, an alternative is to base payroll cost distributions on a periodic time study that monitors employee hours spent on various activities.

In particular, the payroll costs associated with supervision and engineering are to be charged to specific utility functions.

EXAMPLE

Jeff Sutton is a mid-level supervisor. In his most recent week of activities, he worked 20 hours overseeing tree trimming work (classified as maintenance of overhead lines), while also spending 10 hours reviewing line patrol activities (classified as overhead line expenses), and working for 10 hours on general utility administrative activities (classified as administrative and general salaries). Mr. Sutton is paid $45/hour. Based on this information, the cost of his time and his work allocations result in the following journal entry:

Account	Account Description	Debit	Credit
593	Maintenance of overhead lines	900	
583	Overhead line expenses	450	
920	Administrative and general salaries	450	
242	Payroll		1,800

The accounting becomes more complex when utility employees engage in activities that should be charged to more than one account. While the hours associated with these activities can be accumulated by employees on their time sheets, an alternative is to charge the hours based on predetermined percentages.

EXAMPLE

An employee spends 40 hours in a safety training class. These hours are proportionally charged to the three activities in which the employee normally engages, on the grounds that the safety training allows the employee to perform these three activities more safely.

Labor Loadings

Labor loadings involve the systematic allocation of specific types of indirect labor costs and non-productive labor. Examples of indirect labor costs are group insurance, pensions, unemployment insurance, and social security taxes – essentially any expense paid by a utility on behalf of its employees. Examples of non-productive labor are sick pay, holiday pay, and vacation pay, as well as time lost due to bad weather and equipment failures. Since these costs cannot be directly associated with any specific activities, they are allocated to those accounts to which productive labor is charged. For example, the social security taxes associated with the wages paid for labor hours spent on capital projects are assigned to the same projects. The accounting treatment is somewhat different for operating activities, however, where the associated social security taxes are instead charged to one of the 408 sub-accounts, *Taxes – U.S. Social Security – FICA*.

The accrued amount of these costs is then recorded in account 242, *Miscellaneous Current and Accrued Liabilities*. When expenditures for these indirect labor costs and non-productive labor are incurred, the amounts actually incurred are charged against account 242, thereby reducing the amount of the outstanding liability.

Labor loadings are usually applied as a proportion of the direct labor cost of the labor charged to each account. The proportion is derived from the ratio of historical costs of indirect labor costs and non-productive labor to the total productive labor cost.

EXAMPLE

A utility applies employee benefit costs and non-productive labor costs to its productive labor accounts based on the actual proportions of these costs in the preceding year, when they were 11% and 17% of productive labor costs, respectively. The labor loading for four of the labor accounts appears in the following table.

Account	Description	Amount	Employee Benefit Labor Load (11%)	Non-Productive Labor Load (17%)	Loaded Amount
581	Load dispatching	$10,000	$1,100	$1,700	$2,800
582	Station expenses	32,000	3,520	5,440	8,960
583	Overhead line expenses	47,000	5,170	7,990	13,160
584	Underground line expenses	11,000	1,210	1,870	3,080
	Totals	$100,000	$11,000	$17,000	$28,000

Labor Clearing Accounts

In a utility, labor costs may be initially charged to a labor clearing account, which is a short-term holding account from which the costs are then allocated to other accounts. Labor loadings may be conducted on labor costs within a labor clearing account, or the loadings can be conducted once they have been assigned to other accounts. It is generally more efficient to initially record all labor in a labor clearing account, conduct labor loadings there, and then assign the fully-loaded labor costs to other accounts.

EXAMPLE

A hydroelectric utility records $80,000 of labor expenses, which it initially records in account 184, *Clearing Accounts*. Its accounting department then conducts a labor loading procedure, which results in the balance in account 184 increasing to $107,000. Based on the underlying employee timesheets, the accountants then allocate the balance in account 184 to three maintenance accounts, using the following entry:

Account	Account Description	Debit	Credit
551	Maintenance supervision and engineering	32,000	
552	Maintenance of structures	12,000	
553	Maintenance of generating and electric equipment	63,000	
184	Clearing accounts		107,000

The process of transferring the balances out of labor clearing accounts is usually conducted as part of the period-end closing activities.

Payroll Controls

A useful control is to review the accounts to which employee hours are being charged, to see if there are any anomalies. Generally, employees will charge roughly the same hours to the same accounts from one period to the next, so an outlier entry could indicate that an incorrect entry was made.

Special Topics

There are several smaller accounting topics pertaining to utilities that were not addressed in the preceding discussions, such as the allowance for doubtful accounts, bond transactions, and unbilled revenue. They are covered in the following sub-sections.

Allowance for Doubtful Accounts

A utility should set up a reserve of doubtful accounts. This is needed under the accrual basis of accounting, where any projected uncollectible customer accounts are to be recognized in the same reporting period as the one in which the related revenues are recognized. The allowance is usually calculated based on the historical average rate of actual bad debts to revenues.

EXAMPLE

The Newport Utility experienced a bad debt rate of 2.6% in the past year. Its controller elects to carry this percentage forward in developing the current year's allowance for doubtful accounts. The current month's revenue was $4 million, so the corresponding allowance for the month is recorded as $104,000 (calculated as $4,000,000 revenue × 2.6% bad debt rate). The entry is:

Account	Account Description	Debit	Credit
904	Uncollectible accounts (expense)	104,000	
144	Allowance for doubtful accounts (asset)		104,000

The collections department then finds that an industrial customer has gone bankrupt, so its $5,500 billing will not be collected. This will be recorded with a credit to the accounts receivable account and a debit to the allowance for doubtful accounts, thereby drawing down the balance in this reserve account.

Bond Transactions

Utilities routinely issue bonds in order to fund the purchase of power generating and distribution systems. A utility will incur significant issuance costs whenever it issues bonds, usually for a variety of legal and consulting services that are needed to complete the bond document and sell the bonds to investors. If the utility can recover these costs through utility rates over the life of the bonds, then the issuance costs should initially be recorded as an asset and then amortized over the repayment period.

When a bond is issued with a below-market interest rate as its stated rate, then investors will bid low to buy these bonds, so that their effective interest rate matches the market rate for similar securities. This means that the utility will sell the bonds for less than their face amount. For example, a utility sells a bond with a $1,000 face amount for $980, which results in the following entry:

Account	Account Description	Debit	Credit
131	Cash (asset)	980	
226	Unamortized discount on long-term debt (contra)	20	
221	Bonds payable (liability)		1,000

The discount is then amortized over the life of the bond, so that it is eliminated by the bond's maturity date. The amortization effectively increases the interest expense paid by the utility, so that it matches the market interest rate on the date when the bonds were sold.

Conversely, if the stated rate on a bond is higher than the market rate, then investors will be willing to pay a premium for it, so that their effective interest rate matches the market rate for similar securities. This means that the utility will sell the bonds for more than their face amount. For example, a utility sells a bond with a $1,000 face amount for $1,050, which results in the following entry:

Account	Account Description	Debit	Credit
131	Cash (asset)	1,050	
225	Unamortized premium on long-term debt (contra)		50
221	Bonds payable (liability)		1,000

The premium is amortized over the life of the bond, so that it has been eliminated by the maturity date of the bond.

There are cases in which a utility might elect to buy back its own bonds, usually on the grounds that they are currently trading at a discount to par. Buying them back at a discount generates a gain on the reacquired debt. For example, a utility's bonds, with a face value of $1,000, are trading at $950. The utility buys back 10 bonds and records the following entry:

Account	Account Description	Debit	Credit
221	Bonds payable (liability)	10,000	
131	Cash (asset)		9,500
257	Unamortized gain on reacquired debt (deferred credit)		500

The unamortized gain on this repurchase is then amortized over what would have been the remaining life of the bonds.

Cost Allocations

In keeping with the general concept of applying activity-based costing whenever possible, the recommended FARC operating expenses are to be charged to specific functional areas. Thus, the payroll costs of one supervisor could theoretically be spread across multiple functional areas, if he or she spent time on them. Along the same lines, maintenance costs are to be charged to specific functional areas. There are several other areas within a utility that provide services within the entity. For example, the procurement, human resources, fleet management, internal audit, and information technology functions all provide services to other departments. Some costs of these service departments could be allocated to the departments receiving their services. For example, the cost of running the payroll department could be allocated to other departments based on the number of employees in those departments, on the assumption that each person being paid is causing some payroll costs to be incurred. Similarly, facility costs can be charged to the various departments based on the square footage that they occupy.

Cost Recoveries

In cases where there is a salvage value associated with materials that are recovered from maintenance activities, any amounts realized from their disposition are to be offset against the cost of the related maintenance activity. Along the same lines, the receipts from any sub-leased properties are to be recorded as rent revenue, so that they can be offset against the cost of those properties.

Unbilled Revenue

Under the accrual basis of accounting, a utility should accrue for any unbilled revenue at the end of its reporting period. The most accurate way to do this is to wait until the utility's next billing cycle ends, and then prorate the amount billed to address the number of unbilled days in the reporting period. A significant downside of this approach is that the utility cannot close its books until the next billing cycle has been concluded, which could represent a delay of several weeks.

EXAMPLE

The Henderson Utility closes its billing cycle on the 15th day of each month. Its accounting department is closing the books for the month of June, and so does not have any billing information for the period from June 16 through June 30. Its controller elects to wait until the following billing cycle has closed, which yields a figure of $3 million for the period from June 16 to July 15. She can apply half of this amount to the accrued revenue figure for the month of June, since 15 of the 30 days in the billing cycle were in June.

An alternative way to estimate unbilled revenue is to develop an estimate based on historical information. This approach is much quicker, allowing the books to be closed within a short period of time. However, it will be less accurate than just waiting for the current billing cycle to be completed.

EXAMPLE

The Silverthorne Utility's accounting department accrues revenue based on a rolling average of the revenue generated from its last three billing cycles, with a 50% weighting on the revenue billed in the immediately preceding month. Its billing cycle ends on the 15th day of the month. Its controller compiles the following information for the preceding three months:

	Billed Revenue	Days in Period	Weighting	Weighted Revenue
November	$800,000	31*	25%	$200,000
December	875,000	30*	25%	218,750
January	925,000	31*	50%	462,500
				$881,250

* The number of days in the November billing cycle is 31, since it covers October 16 to November 15. The number of days in the December billing cycle is 30, since it covers November 16 to December 15. The number of days in the January billing cycle is 31 days, since it covers the period December 16 to January 15.

The weighted revenue figure is $881,250 ÷ 30.75 weighted average days = $28,659. Since there are 13 unbilled days in February, the controller accrues $372,567 of revenue for this period (calculated as $28,659 × 13 days).

Utility Rate Design

Much of the accounting for a public utility is based on the underlying concern that the typical utility operates in a monopoly environment. That being the case, a utility could theoretically charge very high rates to its customers with impunity, since they have nowhere else to go. To avoid this situation, government regulators set the rates that utilities can charge to their customers. These rates are intended to be fair and equitable for all parties, where customers pay a reasonable rate while the utility is able to recover its costs and generate a reasonable return on investment. An oversight board usually sets rates.

Arriving at the allowed rates requires a utility to rigidly record its costs in accordance with the Uniform System of Accounts, so that the applicable regulatory body can use this information to calculate the allowable rate.

The rates that a utility is allowed to charge will be derived from an average of its power generating costs. Thus, if it has a diesel generating plant, a wind farm, and an interest in a nuclear facility, the costs of all three will be combined to derive an average power generating cost that will be charged to all customers within that utility's territory. The nature of these costs will vary by utility, but typically the largest cost is fuel, followed by debt service and capital improvement costs, followed by operations and maintenance costs.

The rate setters also consider the effects of weather on a utility's operations, since inclement weather can have a substantial negative impact on the cost of its operations. Rates should also incorporate the variability of fuel prices, which may vary substantially if a utility is forced to acquire some of its fuel needs at spot rates on the open market. In short, the derivation of a utility's rates depends on a firm knowledge of its operating costs, and the extent to which those costs can vary under a variety of conditions.

EXAMPLE

The Sonoma Utility has operating expenses of $42 million, routine ongoing capital additions of $4 million, and debt servicing costs of $3.5 million. Based on this information, the utility's oversight board will need to derive rates that result in revenue for the utility of $49.5 million (which is the sum of the three preceding items).

The rates that a utility will be allowed to charge can be structured in several ways. Rates may vary by time of day, with increased charges during daylight hours in order to discourage electricity use at those times when the utility is operating at close to its peak capacity. In essence, shifting consumers to lower-usage periods allows a utility to invest in less power generating capacity. Another pricing option is to charge more to major users once they exceed a certain usage level, on the grounds that the excess billings are needed to pay for the extra capacity levels needed to service these customers. A utility may also charge pass-through rates, which may vary frequently, based on changes in a utility's fuel or purchased power costs. Each of these approaches is designed to address the cost issues of a utility, either in terms of controlling its fixed costs (with peak period charges) or to recover its variable costs (with pass-through charges). When setting these rates, the oversight board will need to develop a rate structure that does not unduly subsidize some customers at the expense of others.

Another rate system is the rate stabilization reserve. This is a cash set-aside that is funded by a rate increase, and which is apportioned out to a utility whenever it incurs a large spike in its power costs. These spikes are typically due to changes in market rates for purchased power or changes in fuel costs. For example, a utility allocates $5 million of its revenues to a rate stabilization fund in Year 1. In Year 2, the utility incurs an additional $1 million of power costs that it cannot include in its rates, so the utility's oversight board authorizes that $1 million from the reserve can be used to offset these costs.

Summary

The proper accounting for transactions is an essential activity within a public utility, since this information is used to derive a rate structure that is then used to bill customers for their electricity usage. It is essential for the accountant to follow the transaction recordation rules, so that the rates established will be sufficient for a utility to at least recover its costs.

Much of this course has been designed under the assumption that a public utility must adhere to the chart of accounts requirements promulgated by the FERC. This is not always the case, since the FERC rules only apply to larger utilities or investor-owned ones. However, many state and local statutes mandate that standard industry accounting practices be followed, so it is quite likely that most utilities will engage in the accounting practices outlined in this course.

Glossary

A

Accretion expense. The ongoing, scheduled recognition of an expense related to a long-term liability.

Accrual basis of accounting. A recordkeeping methodology under which revenue is recorded when earned and expenses when incurred.

Activity-based costing. A methodology for more precisely allocating overhead costs by assigning them to activities.

Allowance for doubtful accounts. A reserve against bad debts expected to arise in the future.

Amortization. The gradual extinguishment of an amount in an account by distributing it over a fixed period, over the life of the related asset or liability, or over the period when its benefit will be realized.

Asset retirement obligation. The costs that will be incurred in the future to retire an asset from use.

B

Book value. The original cost of an asset, minus all accumulated depreciation and impairment charges.

C

Capital asset. Property that is expected to generate value over a long period of time.

Clearing account. A transitional account that is initially used to store transactions before they can be directed to other accounts.

Continuing property records. Plant records for retirement units and mass property that store information about asset names, locations, in-service dates, and so forth.

Contributed asset. Goods and services received with no payment made in exchange.

D

Deferred inflow of resources. When there is an acquisition of net assets that applies to a future reporting period.

Deferred outflow of resources. When there is consumption of net assets that applies to a future reporting period.

Depreciation. The loss in service value not restored by current maintenance, incurred in connection with the consumption of electric plant.

E

Enterprise fund. A self-supported government fund that sells goods and services to the public for a fee.

41

I

Impairment. A loss in value when the service utility of an asset has significantly and unexpectedly declined.

Intangible asset. An asset that lacks physical substance, is a nonfinancial asset, and has a useful life extending over more than one reporting period.

M

Mass assets. Assets that are homogeneous and interchangeable.

N

Non-mass assets. Specifically identifiable assets that can be tracked separately.

P

Public utility. A business that furnishes an everyday necessity to the public at large.

R

Resource. An item that can be drawn down to provide services to citizens.

Retirement units. Those items of electric plant which, when retired, with or without replacement, are accounted for by crediting their book cost.

S

Salvage value. The amount received for property retired, less any expenses incurred in connection with its sale.

Service utility. The usable capacity that an asset was expected to provide when it was acquired.

Special units. Assets that require special accounting treatment, because of regulatory requirements or industry practice.

U

Uniform system of accounts. An account structure and set of associated account definitions promulgated by the Federal Energy Regulatory Commission, for use by public utilities.

Index